THE DICTATORSHIP OF THE PROLETARIAT

THE DICTATORSHIP OF THE PROLETARIAT

Gerald McIsaac

ISBN: 978-1-952302-75-6 (hc)
ISBN: 978-1-952302-74-9 (sc)
ISBN: 978-1-952302-72-5 (e)

Library of Congress Control Number: 2021923150

INTRODUCTION

August 1, 2021. E Day. Eviction Day. The day that an estimated *eleven million* more Americans are scheduled to join the ranks of the homeless, at least if the landlords have their way. That is the day the moratorium on evictions expires, so that is the day the landlords plan to evict all the tenants who cannot pay their rent.

The wits among the working people respond to this news with that which passes for humour. "The good news it that the federal government has set aside $46 billion for rental assistance. The bad news is that only $3 billion is being spent."

The fact that the tenants are unemployed and also hungry, due in part to the Covid Virus, is of no concern to the landlords. But then the landlords are small time capitalists, "petty bourgeois". The buildings they own represent their invested capitol, and they are determined to harvest the largest possible profit from their investment. That means collecting rent. Those who cannot pay the rent are free to live on the street. Nothing personal. Just business. Just capitalism.

Capitalism is precisely the problem. The capitalists are concerned with their profit, their "bottom line". Their goal in life is to make some "serious money", as they phrase it. The health and general well being of the "common people", the "little guy", the "rank and file", the working class, the "masses"—a term I hate, as it sounds so impersonal—are of no concern to the capitalist. For precisely that reason, it is capitalism which has to be abolished and replaced with socialism.

This is not to say that the capitalists are indifferent, concerning the eviction of so many working people. On the contrary, they are quite excited about this. They see this as an "opportunity", and the capitalists are constantly looking for opportunities. It is an opportunity to make a huge profit, so that many capitalists are now investing their capital in real estate. The evictions of so many working people can only work in favour of the capitalists!

The fact of the matter is that capitalism crushes and exploits all common people. Many such people are completely degraded, reduced to the level of beggars, relying on hand outs, merely to survive. All too often, they "self medicate", through the use, and abuse, of alcohol and drugs. That is "one side of the coin", so to speak.

The other side of the coin is the fact that, every so often, people get into motion. Serious motion, if you will excuse the expression. Revolutionary motion, to be precise. This is to say that millions of common people rise up and demand change. We are currently living in a time of revolutionary motion. People are fed up. There are limits. Those who were formerly apathetic are now "waking up", as they phrase it. Now is the time for change. Now is the time for socialism.

It is for the benefit of those who are just now "waking up", taking an interest in their lives, becoming politically active, demanding change, that I have chosen to write this little article. For that reason, certain important scientific terms are explained. Those who are already familiar with those terms may find this tiresome. Bear in mind that due to the revolutionary motion, from among the countless people who are just now becoming politically active, leaders are bound to emerge. It is necessary to prepare them for socialism. After all, it is the most advanced workers, who will form the vanguard of the proletariat, and we can count upon them to lead the proletariat to socialism.

I say this because the one and only alternative to capitalism is "scientific socialism", in the form of the "Dictatorship Of the Proletariat". Common people just have to be made aware of that.

CHAPTER 1
DEFINITION OF CLASSES

Perhaps the first thing our freshly minted revolutionaries are going to have to learn, is that of the existence of classes. In North American, it is customary to deny the existence of classes, or at least that used to be the custom. No doubt the more advanced workers will check for a proper definition, on the internet. It is a wonderful invention, so why not use it?

With that in mind, our rising revolutionary star will learn the following: "Social classes are hierarchial groupings of individuals that are usually based on wealth, educational attainment, occupation, income or membership in a sub culture or social network." It goes on to say that "Many Americans recognize a three tier model that includes the upper class, the middle class, and lower or working class". In scientific jargon, we refer to this as the capitalist, or "bourgeois", definition of classes.

This stands in contrast to that which the internet defines as the "Marxist" definition of a class, which is defined as "a group with intrinsic tendencies and interests that differ from those of other groups within society". If nothing else, it gives common people a place to start.

The internet also reports that most Americans believe that there are three classes in America, as previously listed. This is no doubt a step forward from several years ago, at which time the existence of classes was denied. Then, at around the time of the Occupy Movement, the working people began to sense the existence of classes. They began to refer to themselves as the "99 percent", as opposed to the "1 percent". The understanding, at that time rather vague, was that the working people formed the vast majority of the population, the 99 percent, while the "super rich", the 1 percent, formed the tiny minority. There is some truth to this, and it was a step on the road to class consciousness.

Since that time, the working class has advanced a little farther. Now it is widely understood that working people who are able to make ends meet are "middle class", the poverty stricken are "lower" or "working class", while the "super rich" or billionaires, are "upper class". Although still not completely accurate, it is a step forward from the understanding of "99 percent" versus "1 percent". The latest "three tier model" at least acknowledges the existence of classes.

Much as I personally hate to refer to members of the working class, the proletariat, as "lower class", it is a term which is deeply entrenched in literature, as well as in common usage. In much the same way, I hate to refer to the "super rich", the monopoly capitalists, the "bourgeoisie", as members of the "upper class". Yet that expression also is deeply entrenched, so that there is nothing I can do about it. That merely leaves the middle class, or "petty bourgeois".

In fact, those of us who work for wages are working class, or "proletarians". We have nothing to sell but our labour power. By contrast, the people who own all the factories, mills, mines, railroads, airlines, shipping lines and everything else of any considerable value, are referred to as capitalists, and they are members of a class of people known as the "bourgeoisie". The capitalists make their profit from our labour, so it is in their interests to pay their workers as little as possible, while forcing us to work as hard as possible. It is in the interest of the workers to sell ourselves for the highest possible price. This is to say that the interests of the capitalists, the bourgeois, and the interests of the workers, the proletariat, are "diametrically opposed". That which is in the best interest of one class, is in the worst interest of the other class.

These scientific terms I have placed in quotation marks, as it is important that all working people should learn their meaning. Otherwise, the capitalists will not hesitate to use our lack of awareness of these terms, against us.

That leaves only the members of the middle class, referred to as "petty bourgeois". These people tend to be owners of small businesses, in that such a business is not part of a corporate monopoly. By and large, they are living on "borrowed time", as the corporations have yet to drive them into bankruptcy. Such businesses could include the corner store, for example, or the family owned farm. All are about to go the way of the dodo bird. The monopoly capitalists, the bourgeoisie, working through their corporations, are doing a fine job of eliminating all competition.

If nothing else, this simplifies the class struggle, especially in America, which is the name by which all citizens of the United States refer to themselves. Out of respect for those people, I have chosen to also refer to them as such.

This is to say that Americans have long since given the nobility, otherwise known as the monarchy, their walking papers. The Queen of England is of no concern to Americans. The peasants, otherwise known as family farmers, are now few and far between. Formerly, at the point where the farmer was no longer able to work the farm, the children would take over. That is no longer the case. The children of farmers know better. There are easier ways to work themselves into bankruptcy. Likewise, the small business owner cannot compete with the monopolies, so that they too are being ruined.

This is another way of saying that the class struggle is now sharp and clear. Very simple. Us against them. The workers versus the capitalists. The proletariat battling the bourgeoisie. No holds barred. No quarter. Winner takes it all. War to the finish.

CHAPTER 2

SCIENTIFIC SOCIALISM

Now we have established the fact of the existence of two main classes, the proletariat and the bourgeoisie, as well as the fact that there is a war raging between them. This war has been raging for perhaps three hundred years, ever since the industrial revolution gave birth to those two classes, the bourgeoisie and the proletariat. After all, one class cannot exist without the class opposite to it, or "antipode", as is the correct scientific term. Sometimes this war in hidden, simmering, as it were, and sometimes it flares up into open rebellion. We are very close to the point that the class war will explode into armed conflict. We had best be prepared. This is to say that we had best focus on our goals.

This calls for a little explanation. Some people may find such details tiresome, but bear with me, as it is important.

At the time of the industrial revolution, which started in Great Britain, the class of people known as the burghers, saw an opportunity to invest in factories, mills, mines, railroads, shipping lines and such, and make some money. They succeeded, beyond their wildest dreams. In the process, they became known as bourgeois, a possible corruption of the word burgher, and hired people to work for them, mainly peasants and artisans. These people were transformed into workers, or proletarians, so that two new classes were created.

The capitalists, or bourgeois, knew that they were making a huge profit. They did not know how this was happening, and they really did not care. That is largely true to this day! Their one and only concern is with their profit, their "bottom line", as they phrase it. Yet the economists of the day were concerned, but could not figure it out. With the exception of Karl Marx.

It was Marx, along with his friend and fellow scientist Fredrich Engels, who first conducted a scientific examination of capitalism. This stands in stark contrast to several other "utopian socialists" of the time, fine fellows one and all, who attempted to create socialism, in their own way, under capitalism.

Perhaps the most famous, at least in Great Britain, was Robert Owen, a British industrialist, who lived from 1771 to 1858. He truly cared about people, especially the folks who worked for him. He believed, as all utopian socialists believe, that the best way to enact change, is by first changing moral values and external conditions. With that in mind, he set up a textile manufacturing plant in a place referred to as New Lenark, in Scotland. His goal was to create a community in which "workers were paid what they were worth, and shared everything".

No one can find fault with his ambition. Such a cause is to be admired. There were several other individuals, also utopian socialists, who conducted similar experiments in Europe, at around the same time. All of these experiments ended in failure, through no fault of the socialists. It is simply not possible to create socialism, under capitalism.

This has not stopped other utopian socialists from attempting to create similar socialist societies. Senator Sanders of Vermont, who describes himself as an Independent Socialist, is perhaps the most famous, and certainly well respected. He is also just as mistaken as Owen. In time, he and his followers will find that we can live under capitalism or socialism, but not both, not at the same time.

My point is that it was Marx who conducted a scientific examination of capitalism, and explained how the capitalists made their profit. More than that, he determined a few other things, but perhaps it would be best to allow Marx to explain this, in his own words. In a letter to Weydemeyer, dated March 5, 1852, he stated: "And now as to myself, no credit is due to me for discovering the existence of classes in modern society, nor yet the struggle between them. Long before me, bourgeois historians had described the historical development of this class struggle, and bourgeois economists the economic anatomy of the classes. What I did that was new was to prove: 1) that the *existence of classes* is only bound up with *particular historical phases in the development of production;* 2) that the class struggle necessarily leads to the *Dictatorship Of the Proletariat;* 3) that this dictatorship itself only constitutes the transition to the *abolition of all classes and to a classless society.*"

I should add that I have chosen to place capitols on the Dictatorship Of the Proletariat, as I consider it to be of such vital importance. After all, it is the "touchstone" of a true Marxist.

So now we have a goal upon which to focus. This is vitally important, as there are a great many socialists, including those who claim to be Marxists, who maintain that the class struggle is at the core of Marx's theory. It is not. But from this error springs the distortions, the falsifications, in order to make it acceptable to the bourgeoisie. The people who distort the Marxism are completely devoid of principle, referred to as "opportunists". They are careful to call for only that which the bourgeoisie find to be acceptable. The class struggle is acceptable to the bourgeoisie. The Dictatorship Of the Proletariat is absolutely not acceptable.

Lenin made this quite clear in his work State And Revolution. As he stated. "The theory of the class struggle was *not* created by Marx, but by the bourgeoisie *before* Marx, and generally speaking is *acceptable* to the bourgeoisie. Those who recognize *only* the class struggle are not yet Marxists; these may be found to have gone no further than the boundaries of bourgeois reasoning and bourgeois politics. To limit Marxism to the theory of the class struggle means curtailing Marxism, distorting it, reducing it to something which is acceptable to the bourgeoisie. A Marxist is one who *extends* the acceptance of the class struggle to the acceptance of the Dictatorship Of the Proletariat. This is where the profound difference lies between a Marxist and an ordinary petty (and even big) bourgeois. This is the touchstone on which the *real* understanding and acceptance of Marxism should be tested." (italics by Lenin)

No doubt the members of the working class who have just recently "woken up", become politically active, are bound to be confused by the numerous "Leftist" organizations and political parties. Incidentally, the term Leftist is used in reference to anything which is thought to favour the working class. Also, some political parties claim to be Marxist, while others may claim to be socialist, but not Marxist.

The important thing to remember is that the political parties which claim to be Marxist, but deny the necessity of the Dictatorship Of the Proletariat, are "social chauvinists", socialists in words, chauvinists in deeds. They are defending the bourgeoisie, not to be trusted. We cannot work with them, although there is hope for the rank and file members. The leaders of such parties are almost certainly well aware of the revolutionary theories of Marx and Lenin, and equally well determined to distort those theories. There is no point is trying to reason with them, as they are devoted servants of the bourgeoisie.

By contrast, the parties and groups which claim to be socialist, but not Marxist, we can work with. It matters not if they call themselves Independent Socialists, or Social Democrats, or Democratic Socialists or just plain socialists. They are fighting for socialism, or at least reforms under capitalism. Bear in mind that reforms "strengthen and further the revolutionary movement", according to Marx, so that we can absolutely work with them. But then again, we must still be allowed to put forward our own beliefs in revolution and the subsequent Dictatorship Of the Proletariat. That is a necessary condition for our involvement with them.

CHAPTER 3

DEMOCRACY: BOURGEOIS AND PROLETARIAN

Perhaps we should start by stating that the state apparatus, commonly referred to as the government, came into existence only with the appearance of the first classes. Of course those two classes were slaves and slave owners. As the slaves had a rather annoying habit of rebelling, it was necessary for the slave owners to devise a system of keeping the slaves in their place. With that in mind, the slave owners created a body of armed men. It was their duty to hunt down and capture any escaped slaves, and to crush any slave uprising. In this manner, the first state apparatus was formed. For the slaves it was a dictatorship, as they had no rights, but for the slave owners, it was a democracy.

Over the years, different forms of state apparatus have evolved, as different classes have evolved. Yet all forms of state apparatus serve the same purpose. It is the method one class, the ruling class, uses to suppress all subordinate classes. That is true to this day. In America, the capitalists, the bourgeoisie, are the ruling class, and their method of rule is that of the democratic republic.

As anyone who has recently watched the news can testify, the journalists are focused on the "events of January 6", which they refer to as the "one six insurrection". As I have previously documented, it is certainly true that a window was broken, and apparently a police officer was knocked to the ground. If that is their idea of an insurrection, then they are about to receive a rude awakening! Of course, the capitalists are terrified, as on that day, a great many peaceful protesters -along with a few vandals- marched on the capitol, walked into the government building, almost unopposed, and terrified the politicians. In the process, they exposed the weakness of the capitol.

Of course the journalists are giving their own "spin" to the story. At first, the protesters were accused of being "anarchists", in the service of Donald Trump, as they are convinced that "Trump won the election". The journalists refer to this as the "Big Lie". They could not make that "stick", as it was pointed out to them that anarchists are determined to have no government. As the protesters were determined to reinstate Trump as president, they could not possibly be anarchists.

So now the journalists have "changed their tune". They are now saying that the "one six insurrection" was a "threat to democracy". This is closer to the truth. In fact, it is a threat to democracy, the democracy of the capitalists, "bourgeois democracy". Such little details the journalists neglect to mention.

I am sure our "newly awakened", politically active members of the working class are suspicious -or at least I so hope and pray- and I am equally sure you will be checking with the internet. I too conducted such a search. The response of my search for a definition of democracy was much as I anticipated: “a system of government by the whole population or all the elegible members of a state, typically through elected representatives”. That is very close to the definition of democracy which is taught in schools, that of “majority rule”.

The Marxist understanding of democracy is not quite so “cut and dried”. Lenin explains this quite well in his work, State and Revolution: “In capitalist society, under the conditions most favourable to its development, we have more or less complete democracy in the democratic republic. But this democracy is always restricted by the narrow framework of capitalist exploitation, and consequently always remains, in reality, a democracy for the minority, only for the possessing classes, only for the rich. Freedom in capitalist society always remains about the same as it was in the ancient Greek republics: freedom for the slave owners. Owing to the conditions of capitalist exploitation, the modern wage slaves are also so crushed by want and poverty that ‘they cannot be bothered with democracy’, ‘they cannot be bothered with politics’; in the ordinary peaceful course of events the majority of the population is debarred from participating in social and political life.”

That is, without doubt, a more accurate, detailed description of democracy, a far cry from the “majority rule” of popular belief. The discrepancy can be explained by the fact that the capitalists own the internet, just as they own all the major news outlets, so that all information, including breaking news as well as definitions, are biased in favour of the capitalists.

Yet the fact remains that under the “democratic republic”, we have “more or less complete democracy”. This democracy is “restricted by the narrow framework of capitalist exploitation”, so that it remains a democracy “for the rich”. We refer to this democracy, under capitalism, as "bourgeois democracy". It is a democracy for the bourgeois, but a dictatorship for the proletariat.

It should also be pointed out that there is a big difference between a republic and a country which recognizes a monarch. A republic does not recognize any monarch, which is to say a king or queen, so that the United States is a democratic republic. By contrast, Canada does recognize the Queen of England as the Head of State, the Queen of Canada. Canada is a Constitutional Monarchy.

As I have documented, in a previous article, some of the ways in which democracy is curtailed in America, there is no need to repeat it here. Suffice it to say that it is the members of the Electoral College who elect the President and the Vice President, not the voters. Democracy is also curtailed in Canada, only in a different manner.

As previously mentioned, Queen Elizabeth of England is our Head of State. She is in turn represented in Canada by a Governor General, in this case Mary Simon. It is Mary Simon whom in turn chooses the Canadian head of government, in our case the Prime Minister, and she has the power to act as a restraint on the power of the Prime Minister. According to the internet -a most valuable source of information, however biased- her responsibilities include "carrying out constitutional duties, serving as Commander in Chief, representing Canada at home and abroad, encouraging excellence, and bringing Canadians together".

Perhaps there is some confusion concerning the "state", as opposed to the "government". Most people consider them to be the same, different names for one entity. But as Her Majesty is the Queen of Canada, our Head of State, but not part of our government, they cannot be the same.

In order to provide some clarity, I checked with the internet. They provided their own definition: "The state is the organization, while the government is the particular group of people, the administrative bureaucracy that controls the state apparatus at a given time. That is, governments are the means through which state power is employed". Now we know.

In the case of Canada, the state organization, or "machine", has been set up by the nobility and the capitalists, the bourgeoisie, in order to crush and exploit the common people, the working class. The precise individuals who serve in any capacity, at any given time, may vary from one year to the next, or at best from one election to the next. They form the "government", but regardless of the name of the political party, all serve the same class or classes, in our case the nobility and the bourgeoisie.

As an example, let us assume that the Conservatives have a majority in Parliament, so that the Prime Minister is a member of the Conservative Party. Let us further assume that at the time of a federal election, a different political party, perhaps the Liberals, managed to achieve a majority in Parliament. At that point, it is the duty of the Governor General to appoint a new Prime Minister, a member of the Liberal Party, as the new Prime Minister. The new Prime Minister could then be expected to appoint her cronies, "party faithful", to key positions within the "new government". This includes members of the Cabinet, for example. Different government, different faces, same state apparatus, serving the same capitalist class, crushing the same working class.

As Marx phrased it, federal elections allow the working class to "decide once in every three or six years which member of the ruling class was to misrepresent the people in parliament". Which in no way lessens the importance of the federal elections. It stands as an "index of maturity of the working class." For that reason, if for no other, it is of vital importance to vote in all elections.

Here we have another fine example of democracy which is "restricted". Just as Americans do not elect their President, so too Canadians do not elect their Prime Minister. That little detail is covered by the Governor General, the same lady whose job it is to "bring us together". Now that is a tall order! If there is any group of people who are more divided than the Americans, it is the Canadians!

This is significant, because it is just a matter of time before the revolution breaks out in America. Then it will almost certainly spread to Canada. The two countries have a great deal in common. It is very likely that both countries will form separate independent socialist republics, so that Canadians will finally kiss the British Queen good bye! It cannot happen too soon! It is also quite possible that areas of both countries will unite. That remains to be seen, and is completely up to the people who live in those areas. Yet two examples come immediately to mind. The fact is that northern New England has a great deal in common with the Maritime Provinces, just as Alaska has a great deal in common with the Yukon Territory. The idea that those areas could merge, into separate socialist republics, is quite conceivable.

This brings us to the subject of our next chapter, that of paving the way for the Dictatorship Of the Proletariat, through the destruction of the bourgeois state apparatus.

CHAPTER 4

THE SMASHING OF THE EXISTING STATE APPARATUS

In the last chapter we documented that democracy under capitalism, the rule of the bourgeoisie, is always restricted, twisted, distorted. Our goal, the goal of Marxists, is to establish democracy for the vast majority, the common people, the working class, the proletariat. This can only be accomplished through the Dictatorship Of the Proletariat.

This may at first sound like an "oxymoron", a contradiction in terms. How can a dictatorship be democratic? Yet we have already established that a democracy is merely a method of class rule, that of one class over another class. Under the current American bourgeois democratic republic, it is the bourgeois that rule, so that it is a democracy for the bourgeoisie, but a dictatorship over the proletariat.

The state apparatus which has been set up by the bourgeoisie, with the express purpose of crushing and exploiting the vast majority of people, the working class, the proletariat, must be smashed. This state apparatus includes the police, the standing army, the bureaucracy, the prisons and other coercive institutions. It must be replaced by a different state apparatus, a proletarian state apparatus, with the goal of crushing the desperate and determined resistance of the bourgeois. Rest assured, after the socialist revolution, the resistance of the bourgeoisie will be increased ten fold, as they attempt to restore their "paradise lost". They will resort to any subterfuge, any lie, any deception, to subvert the newly created democratic republic- the Dictatorship Of the Proletariat- and return to power.

Marx was supremely well aware of this, as he was born into the middle class, the petty bourgeois. As was Engels, for that matter. Yet both turned their backs upon a comfortable middle class life style and devoted their lives to the service of the common people. Those who are prejudiced against the middle class intellectuals would do well to bear this in mind!

As social scientists, they determined that society develops according to certain laws. After years of careful study of capitalism, Marx and Engels wrote the Communist Manifesto, in 1848. It gave the working class people of all countries a proper direction. Yet it was not until 1871 that the working people of Paris rose up and formed the Paris Commune. For the first time in history, a working class, proletarian government took shape. This provided Marx with the information he needed, as he had no idea, until that time, of the precise form that the Dictatorship Of the Proletariat should take. But perhaps it would be best to allow Lenin to explain the significance, that of the Paris Commune, as he stated in State and Revolution:

"Marx, however, was not only enthusiastic about the heroism of the Communards who 'stormed the heavens', as he expressed it. Although it did not achieve its aim, he regarded the mass revolutionary movement as a historic experiment of gigantic proportions, as an advance of the world proletarian revolution, as a practical step that was more important than hundreds of programs and discussions. Marx conceived his task to be to analyze this experiment, to draw lessons in tactics from it, to reexamine his theory in the light it afforded.

"Marx made the only 'correction' he thought it necessary to make in the Communist Manifesto on the basis of the revolutionary experience of the Paris Communards.

"The last preface to the new German edition of The Communist Manifesto, signed by both its authors, is dated June 24, 1872. In this preface the authors, Karl Marx and Frederich Engels, say that the program of the Communist Manifesto 'has in some details become antiquated' now, and they go on to say: 'One thing especially was proved by the Commune, viz., *that the working class cannot simply lay hold of the ready made state machinery and wield it for its own purposes*'"(italics by Lenin)

This is of vital importance, especially now that the American revolution could break out at any day. The American revolutionaries must not repeat the mistakes of the revolutionary workers of Paris, those who took part in the Paris Commune! The biggest mistake they made was in *not* smashing the existing state machine! Instead, they tried to take over the existing state machine, and use it for their own purposes! Yet the state machine has been carefully designed by the capitalists, for the express purpose of crushing the working class. It stands to reason that the people who manage to take control of that state machine, will inevitably end up using it, for that same purpose! Unless that state machine is smashed, the revolution will succeed only in replacing one set of rulers with another! Out of the frying pan, into the fire!

This helps to explain the rather "peculiar" behaviour of the social chauvinists. They claim to be Marxists, and in fact, tend to be supremely well educated, aware of the revolutionary theories of Marx and Lenin. They are also well aware that those revolutionary theories are correct, that revolution is about to break out, and soon. As they also have the ideology of the capitalist, they see the revolution as an "opportunity". It is simply a matter of pretending to be a Marxist, establishing themselves as leaders of the working class, and at the time of the revolution, setting themselves up as the new rulers, perhaps even as the first "Marxist" President! We already had a first Black President, so why not a Marxist President?

Yet if the working people, those who are taking part in the revolution, manage to mount a successful insurrection, storm the capitol and smash the existing state apparatus -God forbid!- then the juicy political plums, such as the presidency, will be lost forever! For that reason, the working people must not be made aware of the revolutionary theories of Marx and Lenin. Logic of the social chauvinists! There is a method to their madness!

No doubt there are a great many people who scoff at revolutionary theory. They tend to take great pride in their actions, properly so. Yet perhaps they should take to heart the advice of Engels, which is that "without a revolutionary theory, there can be no revolutionary motion".

It may help to think of the working class, the proletariat, as an army at war, which is precisely the case. The enemy is the capitalists, the bourgeoisie. They are also very strong, deeply entrenched. But then they have had many years to prepare their defences. Now the general in charge of the attacking proletarian forces would do well to focus on a clear objective. Otherwise the proletarian forces would end up scattered, disorganized, possibly even fighting each other! By contrast, the proletarian general who focuses her attacks, sending her troops against a specific target, is far more likely to be successful. The ultimate goal is of vital importance. It is important to "keep your eye on the ball". In this case, the "ball", the ultimate goal, is the Dictatorship Of the Proletariat. This goal can only be reached by first smashing the existing state apparatus.

CHAPTER 5
THE PROLETARIAN REVOLUTION AND THE RENEGADE KAUTKSY

Lenin also had his hands full with the social chauvinists. Immediately after the Russian revolution of November 7, 1917, the most advanced strata of the proletariat, in many countries of the world, embraced the Dictatorship Of the Proletariat. In response to this, the capitalists and social chauvinists launched a most vicious campaign of slander and distortion. Perhaps the most skillful of these was a former Marxist, a highly respected individual by the name of Karl Kautsky. His pamphlet, The Dictatorship of the Proletariat, stands to this day as a masterful distortion of Marxism. As the American working class becomes familiar with the Dictatorship Of the Proletariat, we can expect the American bourgeoisie, as well as the American social chauvinists, to sing the praises of Kautsky. For that reason, it is best to give a little historical background.

In his early days, Kautsky was a superb Marxist. Yet that was at a time of relative peace, in the sense that the so called "Great Powers", by which was meant the most highly industrialized countries of the world, were preparing to destroy each other.

These "great predatory powers" were involved in a "rivalry in conquest", as by the second decade of the twentieth century, the whole world had been divided up between them. The British were quite proud of the fact that "the sun never sets on the British Empire". They bragged of this constantly. This merely had the effect of "rubbing salt into the wound", as the Germans, in particular, felt cheated. They had far fewer colonies than Britain, and thought it best to "level the playing field". With that in mind, two huge world alliances took shape, one led by Britain, and the other led by Germany. Britain and her friends became known as the Allied Powers, and included France, Italy, America, Russia, Romania, Japan and their colonies. The opposing world power, led by Germany, included Austro-Hungary, Bulgaria, the Ottoman Empire, and their colonies. They became known as the Axis Powers. The Axis was determined to secure more colonies, while the Allies were determined to hang on to the colonies they had, and preferably add to them. It was a war to redivide the world, and has gone down in history as World War 1. Caught in the middle were the common people, the workers and peasants. They were the "cannon fodder", and were sacrificed, by the millions.

In 1914, at the outbreak of the "Great Imperialist Slaughter", the tension reached a fever pitch. The monopoly capitalists, the "imperialists", the bourgeoisie, of each warring country, were calling for the "defence of the fatherland". Most of the Marxists, those whom had previously been so zealously calling for revolution and the subsequent Dictatorship Of the Proletariat, collapsed under pressure. They largely converted to social chauvinism, those who are socialists in words, chauvinists in deeds. That included Karl Kautsky, a man who has since gone down in history as the "Benedict Arnold" of Marxism. As mentioned earlier, his pamphlet, The Dictatorship of the Proletariat, was widely praised by the capitalists of the time. As very soon the American proletariat will also be discussing the forth coming revolution and the subsequent Dictatorship Of the Proletariat, no doubt the American capitalists will also be singing the praises of Kautsky. For that reason, it is perhaps best to discuss his pamphlet in more detail.

It was Lenin who responded to the "revisionist" efforts of Kautsky, with his own pamphlet, The Proletarian Revolution and the Renegade Kautsky.

As an aside, we should add that a "revisionist" is one who attempts to revise the revolutionary theories of Marx and Lenin. Bear in mind that both Marx and Engels lived in the age of competitive capitalism, at a time in which capitalism had certain progressive features. The age of monopoly capitalism, referred to as "imperialism", appeared at around the beginning of the twentieth century, and has absolutely no progressive characteristics. The characteristics of imperialism were documented by Lenin, quite clearly, in his landmark work, Imperialism, the Highest Stage of Capitalism.

Lenin documented the revisionist heresies of Kautsky in the following manner: "Kautsky's pamphlet, The Dictatorship of the Proletariat . . . is a most lucid example of that utter and ignominious bankruptcy of the Second International about which all honest socialists in all countries have been talking for a long time. The proletarian revolution is now becoming a practical issue in a number of countries, and an examination of Kautsky's renegade sophistries and his complete renunciation of Marxism is therefore essential."

It is also a fact that the "proletarian revolution" is once again a "practical issue in a number of countries", and it is once again "essential" to examine his "renegade sophistries and his complete renunciation of Marxism". The reason for this is quite simple. The social chauvinists are quite predictable. They can be expected to rehash the same old garbage which has been spewed out many years ago. They will extol the book of Kautsky as a model of Marxist literature, as a "clarification" of the scientific theories of Marx.

Lenin make this quite clear when he went on to state: "Kautksy . . . is a most typical and striking example of how a verbal recognition of Marxism has led in practice . . . into a bourgeois liberal theory recognizing the non revolutionary "class" struggle of the proletariat . . . By means of patent sophistry, Marxism is stripped of its revolutionary spirit; *everything* is recognized in Marxism *except* the revolutionary methods of struggle, the propaganda and preparation of those methods, and the education of the masses in this direction. Kautsky 'reconciles' in an unprincipled way the fundamental idea of social chauvinism . . . The working class cannot play its world revolutionary role unless it wages a ruthless struggle against this backsliding, spinelessness, subservience to opportunism, and unparalleled vulgarization of the theories of Marxism"

As is well known, at the time this article was written, a number of countries, especially in western Europe, were ripe for revolution. Yet that revolution never took place, if only because the working people were deprived of their leaders. Most of the Marxists took the lead of Kautsky and became social chauvinists, devoted servants of the capitalists. There were notable exceptions, such as Rosa Luxemburg and Karl Liebnecht of Germany, fine Marxists, people of principle. As such, the capitalists recognized them as the threat they were, and had them murdered.

Modern day Marxists, otherwise known as Communists, would do well to bear this in mind. While putting forth the revolutionary theories of Marx and Lenin, they would be well advised to take reasonable precautions.

It is true that in various countries of western Europe, numerous uprisings took place. These were isolated and scattered incidents, lacked focus and direction, as there were no Marxist leaders to provide the proper direction. This merely confirms the advice of Engels, to the effect that "without a proper revolutionary theory, there can be no revolutionary motion". Americans would do well to bear that in mind!

We now have some fine tools, as modern technology has provided us with various electronic digital devices, as well as the internet. We can use these to communicate with each other, as well as countless working people. The "perverts", including child molesters and human traffickers, manage to stay in touch, using something referred to as the "dark net", so it can clearly be done.

We can expect the capitalists to perpetuate the myth of "pure democracy", as opposed to a dictatorship, and in particular the Dictatorship Of the Proletariat. It is the duty of true Marxists, Communists, to make the working class aware that of the fact that pure democracy is an oxymoron, a contradiction in terms. Democracy is merely a state apparatus, a method by which one class suppresses, crushes, another class. There is nothing "pure" about a class being crushed! Under bourgeois democracy, the tiny class of the minority, the capitalists, the bourgeoisie, rules. They in turn crush the vast majority, the working class, the proletariat. They also exploit the proletariat. It is democracy for the bourgeoisie, but a dictatorship for the proletariat.

By contrast, under the Dictatorship Of the Proletariat, the working class, the proletariat, rules. They in turn crush the tiny minority of capitalists, the bourgeoisie. For the vast majority, the proletariat, it is a democracy, but for the tiny minority of former exploiters, the bourgeoisie, it is a dictatorship.

As explained in a previous article, most American working people can read, and have access to digital devices. This is not to say they those same workers are "Philadelphia lawyers", as they are not. So this has to be explained to them, in terms they can understand.

Now when the capitalists refer to democracy, which is a method of class rule, our response must be, "democracy for which class?"

Bear in mind that Lenin refers to the Dictatorship Of the Proletariat as the "very essence of proletarian revolution". He goes on to say that "This is a question that is of the greatest importance for all countries, especially for the advanced ones, especially for those at war, and especially at the present time. One may say, without fear of exaggeration, that this is the key problem of the entire proletarian class struggle. It is therefore, necessary to pay particular attention to it."

We can expect the modern day journalists, devoted servants of the bourgeoisie, one and all, to compare the two "methods", "democratic" with the "dictatorial". We can count on them to not distinguish between the social chauvinists and the true Marxists, the Communists. Just because the social chauvinists refer to themselves as Marxists, does not make it true! Yet no doubt the journalists will sing the praises of the social chauvinists, the Benedict Arnolds of Marxism. They will be praised as the more "moderate elements", "true democrats", as opposed to those who call for the Dictatorship Of the Proletariat.

Our response, in every possible situation, must be to stress the fact that democracy is a method of class rule. There is no "pure democracy", any more than there is any "democracy in general".

Further, proletarian democracy is far superior to bourgeois democracy. The one and only form of proletarian democracy lies in the Dictatorship Of the Proletariat. At each and every situation, we must raise the question of *democracy for which class?* At every rally, every demonstration, every political gathering, our posters and banners must raise this question! It is in this manner, and only in this manner, that the working class will become aware of the fact that democracy is a matter of class rule. They will also become aware of the fact that the Dictatorship Of the Proletariat is the very *essence of the doctrine of Marx!*

We can also expect the capitalists, working through their journalists and possibly their social chauvinists, to contrast democracy with a dictatorship. After all, they tend to be completely predictable! Our response must be to point out the obvious, which is that in ancient times, the state of the slave owners was a dictatorship. The slaves had no rights, but of course it was a democracy for the slave owners. Then, as now, a democracy for one class is nothing more than a dictatorship over another class. A democracy is a dictatorship! Under bourgeois democracy, it is democracy for the bourgeois, but a dictatorship over the proletariat. Under proletarian democracy, the Dictatorship Of the Proletariat, it is a democracy for the working class, but a dictatorship over the bourgeoisie.

The social chauvinists may also insist that a dictatorship implies the rule of a single person. It most certainly does not, so it is up to the true Marxists to draw the attention to the existence of classes. It is only in such a manner that the awareness of the working class, the proletariat, can be raised to that of the level of Marxists.

In desperation, they may even resort to accusing the Marxists of threatening to use force to stay in power, as dictatorship implies a rule unrestricted by any laws. This is most emphatically true. In fact, Lenin expressed himself quite clearly on this very point:

"Dictatorship is rule based directly upon force and unrestricted by any law. The revolutionary Dictatorship Of the Proletariat is rule won and maintained by the use of violence by the proletariat against the bourgeoisie, rule that is unrestricted by any law . . . dictatorship presupposes and implies a 'condition', one so disagreeable to renegades, of *revolutionary violence* of one class against another".

The social chauvinists refuse -or are unable?- to face the fact that the capitalists must be overthrown, and that this can only be accomplished through revolution. In no other way can the bourgeois state machine be smashed, and replaced with a proletarian state apparatus, one which has the sole aim of crushing the bourgeoisie. That proletarian state machine is referred to as the Dictatorship Of the Proletariat, and it is *violence* against the bourgeoisie. The necessity of such violence is *particularly* called for by the existence of *militarism and bureaucracy!*

Another popular argument of the social chauvinists, the traitors to Marxism, is that as we have such a huge majority, far more workers than capitalists, then there is no need to crush the bourgeoisie. So why do we need a dictatorship? They would have us believe that after the revolution, all workers and -former-capitalists can unite as brothers. They would have us embrace the fable of "the lion shall lie down with the lamb". Mankind will then enter an "Age of Aquarius", in that "peace and tranquility, equality and understanding" shall reign supreme. That would be so nice! It is not about to happen! It may be written in the stars, according to astrologers, but no where is it engraved in stone, here on planet earth! Even if it is engraved in stone, it remains a barefaced lie!

Feel free to face reality! The fact is that it is possible to *defeat* the oppressors at one stroke, possibly by a successful uprising in the capitol, similar to that which happened on January 6, or "one six", as is the common expression. In such a manner the capitalists will be *overthrown*, but not *destroyed*! Even after the capitalists are deposed, they will still remain *stronger than the proletariat!* Face the facts! Unless they are suppressed, absolutely crushed, they will most certainly *return to power!*

All working people are well aware that no one wants to lower their standard of living. The billionaires are no exception! They are accustomed to living in the "lap of luxury". Servants wait on them "hand and foot". They own houses that can only be described as mansions, regular palaces. As well, they have fleets of luxury vehicles, yachts and even jet aircraft, so that they can fly to any place in the world, at any time, to satisfy any whim. They have never done an honest days work in their lives, certainly not manual labour, and have no intention of starting! Their idea of a joke is to say that "manual labour" is a Spanish peasant! Yet the social chauvinists would have us believe that those are the same people who are going to embrace the Dictatorship Of the Proletariat! Fat chance! There is no way on Gods green earth that they are about to get their hands dirty!

On the contrary, at this moment, meaning before the revolution, the billionaires are not even concerned! It is characteristic of any and all ruling classes, and the capitalists are no exception, to believe that their rule will last forever! It just never occurs to them that they can be overthrown! Such thoughts never cross their mind! And no wonder! They pay their flunkies to worry about such little details!

These flunkies, belly crawling boot lickers, one and all, are paid quite handsomely, to tell the billionaires that which the billionaires want to hear! They earn their pay! They assure the capitalists that "all bases are covered", "there is nothing to worry about", "everything is under control", the sounds from the streets are merely "loud noises". The capitalists believe them!

In fact, the "loud noises" from the streets, are the sounds of revolution! The protests, the marches and demonstrations, are the sound of the working class rising up! The Autonomous Zones, which are springing up across the country are the equivalent to the Soviets, councils of workers! The states which are uniting, in various parts of the country, are about to declare independence and form separate socialist republics! They are also about to tell Washington what they can do with their national debt!

We can expect the American revolution to take the shape of an Insurrection, much as happened on November 7, 1917, in the Russian capitol of Saint Petersburg. At that time, the first socialist republic was formed, a true Dictatorship Of the Proletariat, although in that case they were assisted by the poor peasants. We can also expect the forth coming American revolution to be led by women, as the American proletarian men have not fulfilled their duty. By contrast, the women have proven themselves to be excellent organizers. We can only hope that the men will follow their lead. On that day, the capitalists will learn the meaning of the word Insurrection! It involves something more than breaking a window and knocking down a cop!

On the day of the Insurrection, the first day of the revolution, we can expect the flunkies of the capitalists to have a "conversion", so that they will instantly be converted into die hard revolutionaries. They will abandon the capitalists in droves! They will approach us with outstretched hands, warm smiles on their faces! We in turn must embrace them as the brothers and sisters, the comrades that they are! Their past service to the capitalists must not be held against them! We can use all the help we can get! Besides, the capitalists have trained them well! They have certain skills which, no doubt, will prove to be quite useful!

By contrast, on that day the capitalists will be completely stunned, alone and isolated, for perhaps the first time in their lives. They will cry out in vain for their servants. Slowly, the horrible, sickening realization will dawn on them, the fact that the unimaginable has happened. The unthinkable. The "plebians" have rebelled. The lower classes have revolted. Their whole world, that of luxury and decadence, has just come crashing down.

Most will resist the first mad impulse to end it all, to commit suicide, although a few will succumb to temptation, just as so many Nazis ended their own lives, as the Third Reich came crashing down. The more stalwart will brace themselves for the coming battle, against the Dictatorship Of the Proletariat. They will be determined to restore their "paradise lost", to return to their life of luxury. It is simply a matter of overthrowing the Dictatorship Of the Proletariat.

Lenin had a few words to say, concerning the social chauvinist Kautsky, and his nonsense of "majority rule". As Lenin stated: "In these circumstances, to assume that in a revolution which is at all profound and serious the issue is decided simply by the relation between the majority and minority is the acme of stupidity, the silliest prejudice of a common liberal, an attempt to *deceive the people* by concealing from them a well established historical truth. This historical truth is that in every profound revolution, the *prolonged, stubborn and desperate* resistance of the exploiters, whom for a number of years retain important practical advantages over the exploited, is the *rule.* Never -except in the sentimental fantasies of the sentimental fool Kautsky- will the exploiters submit to the decision of the exploited majority, without trying to make use of their advantages in a last desperate battle, or series of battles." (italics by Lenin)

That is precisely the reason we need the Dictatorship Of the Proletariat! Either we crush the capitalists, the bourgeoisie, or they will return to power!

Lenin goes on to state: "The transition from capitalism to communism takes an entire historical epoch. Until this epoch is over, the exploiters inevitably cherish the hope of restoration, and this *hope* turns into *attempts* at restoration. After their first serious defeat, the overthrown exploiters- whom had not expected their overthrow, never believed it possible, never conceded the thought of it- throw themselves with energy grown ten fold, with furious passion and hatred grown a hundred fold, into the battle for the recovery of the 'paradise', of which they were deprived, on behalf of their families, whom had been leading such a sweet and easy life, and whom now the 'common herd' is condemning to ruin and destitution".

CHAPTER 6

PREPARING FOR THE DICTATORSHIP OF THE PROLETARIAT

Revolutionary situations call for revolutionary measures. The current situation is revolutionary, and this is no exception. No doubt there are countless things which should be done, but it is important to "keep your eye on the ball", or as Lenin phrased it, to focus on the "key link". The key link now is to prepare for the Dictatorship Of the Proletariat.

The level of awareness of the working class must be raised, to the level of that of a true Marxist. More accurately, the most advanced workers must be made aware of the revolutionary theories of Marx and Lenin. These workers are the "vanguard" of the working class, as the less advanced pay strict attention to the opinion of the more advanced.

Marxists must work as closely as possible with the utopian socialists, those who consider themselves to be socialists, but not

Marxists. At the same time, we must distinguish ourselves from the social chauvinists, the Benedict Arnolds of Marxism.

All American citizens should be encouraged to become card carrying members of the two mainstream political parties, Democrat and Republican. As such, they can then run for any and all political office, hopefully flooding Washington with socialists. In the process, they will learn the meaning of "bourgeois democracy". Experience is such a fine teacher!

The creation of "Autonomous Zones" is to be encouraged, but not in the geographical sense. The experience of the Seattle Autonomous Zone has proven that the capitalists will not tolerate any Zones which claim to be Autonomous. They see such Zones as a threat to their rule, which is precisely the case. So such Zones must work "underground". The members must receive military training, including the use of firearms, and prepare for an Insurrection, the first step of the revolution.

The creation of a true Marxist political party is essential, American Communist Party, Dictatorship Of the Proletariat, ACP, DOP. Without such a Party to give the proper direction, it is doubtful that the revolution can succeed.

Make full use of the internet. Take every reasonable precaution. Remember that Rosa Luxemburg was a martyr, and we do not need any more martyrs.

Prepare revolutionary literature for working people. Most such literature is a crashing bore, so try to be entertaining, but by no means vulgar. Bear in mind that the best way to educate people, is by entertaining them at the same time. They are also interested in more than just wages and working conditions, so bear that in mind.

Tailor the literature for the audience. The more advanced workers must receive more advanced literature, while the less advanced must receive more popular literature. No workers must be neglected.

Organize more marches and demonstrations. Harass the capitalists wherever they are. That includes their offices, places of business, homes, vacation resorts and banks. Allow them no peace. Carry posters and banners which call for the Dictatorship Of the Proletariat. As soon as that becomes a popular expression, we will know that it is time to organize an Insurrection.

Socialist Insurrection Imminent

Jun 5, 2021

Within America, the tension is mounting, daily rising to greater levels. Desperation is wide spread. The gun violence is reported to be at "epidemic proportions", with senseless shootings, "mass casualty events", almost on a daily basis. Yet history reveals that Americans are not about to tolerate this. This has been demonstrated in the past. Americans can only be pushed to far.

Around the year 1863, in that which is commonly referred to as the "old west", there was a well organized gang of thieves which was stealing from a group of miners, hard working people, who would dig the ore out of the ground, only to have it stolen. The local law enforcement was stumped, the sheriff unable to track down these outlaws. He was dead set opposed to the creation of any "vigilante committee", as it was up to the law to apprehend these bandits, and bring them to justice. Citizens do not have the right to take the law into their own hands!

Yet the honest, hard working citizens decided that enough was enough, and formed a vigilante committee. They then grabbed a man who always seemed to have money, even though he never worked. They suspected that he was one of the gang, and they were right. The citizens were able to extract information from this man, concerning the identity of the other gang members, led by a man named Plummer, who just happened to be the Sheriff of the town. No wonder he could not catch these outlaws! He was the head of the gang! So the citizens, the vigilantes, grabbed Plummer and perhaps thirty of the gang members, or at least all they could get their hands on, and hung them. Frontier justice. They were strung up from the nearest tree. Other gang members high tailed it out of there, quite horrified that there was no trial, no judge and jury, no lawyers to hide behind. This was an early demonstration of Americans, treating thieves and killers in the proper manner. All of these miners were honest men, some of whom worked their own claims, while others worked for wages. They all did what they had to do, in order to survive.

Now we have a similar situation in America. Once again the thieves and killers are crushing the working class, the proletariat. Only this time the gang is a class, a class of capitalists, the billionaires, the bourgeoisie. Once again we can expect the workers to come together, only this time it will not be as vigilantes, but as a nation wide network, united in their opposition to the capitalists. This network of workers will plan an insurrection, in order to overthrow the capitalists and establish a socialist republic, in the form of the Dictatorship Of the Proletariat.

With that in mind, perhaps a few words from Lenin: "To be successful, insurrection must rely not upon conspiracy and not upon a party, but upon the advanced class. That is the first point. Insurrection must rely upon a *revolutionary upsurge of the people.* That is the second point. Insurrection must rely upon that *turning point* in the history of the growing revolution when the activity of the advanced ranks of the people is at its height, and when the *vacillations* in the ranks of the enemy and *in the ranks of the weak, half hearted and irresolute friends of the revolution* are strongest. That is the third point . . . Once these conditions exist, however, to refuse to treat insurrection as an *art* is a betrayal of Marxism and a betrayal of the revolution." (italics by Lenin)

As yet, we do not have a proper Communist Party, Dictatorship Of the Proletariat, or CP, DOP, but as Lenin said, a successful insurrection does not rely upon a Communist Party. Nor does it rely upon a conspiracy. It relies upon the working class, the proletariat, the one and only advanced American class. A successful insurrection also relies upon a revolutionary upsurge of the people. At the time in which that revolutionary upsurge reaches a peak, and the vacillations within the ranks of the enemy are at the greatest, that is the time for insurrection. That time in now.

Aside from the working class, the proletariat, the only other class of any significance, in opposition to the capitalists, is the middle class, the petty bourgeois. The remnants of that class are under extreme pressure from the monopoly capitalists, the billionaires, and has been recently decimated. So many have been ruined, forced into bankruptcy and the ranks of the proletariat. The remainder are hanging on by their finger tips, waiting for the axe to fall. For that reason, the petty bourgeois tend now to support the proletariat.

The current revolutionary motion is very high, and the capitalist class, the bourgeoisie, is immobilized. Washington is in a state of gridlock. The Democrats and Republicans are at each others throats. The only item they can agree upon now, is to stop Trump. He and a great many of his followers are convinced that he won the election, and are determined to place Trump back in the White House, and soon. His plan is to be in the White House by August of this year.

At the same time, within the country, no less than three independent socialist republics have taken shape, on the east coast, the west coast, and in the industrial heart land of the midwest. Seventeen states so far, and counting. We can expect them to separate any day now. As well, the colonies of Puerto Rico, Alaska and Hawaii will soon declare independence. The stage is set for revolution.

Bear in mind that if Trump manages to get back into power, then the revolution will be much more difficult. The working class has to organize an insurrection, and soon. The only people who have proven themselves capable of this, are the women. The

Women's March of 2017 was a spectacular success. No doubt many millions of people took part that day, mainly women, all across the country. Congratulations ladies, and now it is time to repeat the performance, but on a larger scale. Now it is time to mount a nation wide insurrection. The capitalists have to be overthrown, a socialist republic has to be established, and "fate" has decided that it is up to you ladies to take the bull by the horns. By fate, I mean that the working men have failed to rise to the occasion. It shames me to say that, but it is true.

As I have documented this in a previous article, there is no need to repeat it here. At the same time that an insurrection is being planned and executed, a proper Communist Party must take shape. Those who are familiar with the revolutionary theories of Marx and Lenin, and are interested in scientific socialism, can and must form a Communist Party, Dictatorship Of the Proletariat. Without such a Party to provide the proper leadership, the revolution will almost certainly fail. At the same time, bear in mind that it is not a numbers game. The size of the Party is not nearly as important as the policy it pursues. Allow those who tend to vacillate, to remain in the camp of the vacillators. We have no use for such people, within the Communist Party.

After the insurrection, a new government will be established. It will of necessity be a coalition government, one which represents different classes, the proletariat and the petty bourgeois, as well as different factions within those classes. After all, not everyone embraces the Dictatorship Of the Proletariat.

In Russia of 1917, the situation was far more complicated. The Social Democrats were divided between the Bolsheviks, the party of Lenin, and the Mensheviks, those who tended to be revisionists, those who were of the opinion that the theories of Marx should be revised. The Constitutional Democrats, the Cadets, supported the nobility and the landlords, as the landlords were related, or at least devoted, to the nobility. They also generally supported the capitalists, the bourgeoisie. The Socialist Revolutionaries tended to represent a great many peasants, although they were generally divided between the Left Socialist Revolutionaries, who were close to the Bolsheviks, and the Right Socialist Revolutionaries, who were close to the Cadets. Even within the Bolshevik Party, there was Trotsky and his followers, who did their best to sabotage the revolution.

It did not help that Russia was also at war with Germany and the Central Powers, as well as being surrounded by hostile forces. Any gambler would have offered odds, heavily against a successful revolution. Yet the revolution succeeded, as Lenin was able to persuade so many progressive people, of the correctness of the revolutionary theories of Marx. Perhaps those taking part in the current American revolution, can take inspiration from this.

Immediately after the November 7 insurrection, the Cadets and Mensheviks demanded that the secret treaties of the Czar, with the British and French, be honoured. In this way, they exposed themselves as the strongest supporters of the capitalists. When their demands were refused, they walked out of the assembly. They wanted no part of the new socialist government, which was at that time being created. Good riddance! As well, the Bolsheviks endorsed the agrarian program of the Socialist Revolutionaries. Not that they agreed entirely with it, but had no doubt that the peasants would learn, from experience, that the Bolsheviks were correct. This is referred to as compromise, but not on principle. At no point did the Bolsheviks compromise their principles.

After the American insurrection, we can expect the strongest supporters of the capitalists, to demand that the national debt be honoured. If they cannot prevent the break up of the American empire -and they cannot- then the least they can do is demand that the separate socialist republics pay "their share" of the national debt. Not likely. We can also expect those boot lickers, of the capitalists, to demand that a "democratic republic" be established, along the same lines of the previous republic, with a President, Cabinet, Senate and Congress. Of course the plan of such people is to set themselves up as the new rulers.

It must be explained to working people that such a "democratic republic", is democratic only for the capitalists, the bourgeoisie. It is a government organization, a state apparatus, which was set up by the capitalists, with the idea of crushing the working class, the proletariat. Such a state apparatus must be destroyed and replaced with a working class state apparatus, with the idea of crushing the "desperate and determined" resistance of the billionaires, the bourgeoisie, with their plans to return to power. This state apparatus is referred to as the Dictatorship Of the Proletariat.

With that in mind, all working people should be encouraged to read that most relevant book by Lenin, State and Revolution. He explains this quite clearly, and no doubt working people will find this to be quite enlightening.

We can also expect a popular political party to take shape, in the form of a Social Democratic Party. Those who refer to themselves as independent socialists, or social democrats, can be expected to join this Party. Among the leaders we can expect to find the Senator from Vermont, as well as those who are referred to as the Squad, within the House of Representatives. They are well respected and will no doubt serve with distinction, within the new socialist government.

The Social Democrats are the natural and desirable allies of the proletariat. They are fighting for democracy and socialism. They may, or may not, adhere to the revolutionary theories of Marx and Lenin. That includes the "touchstone" of a true Marxist, the

Dictatorship Of the Proletariat. That is perfectly acceptable, as in time they, or at least the vast majority of the working people, will be convinced of the correctness of our position.

The current situation is revolutionary. The mass movement of the working class, the proletariat, is at a peak. Desperation is gripping the country. The ruling class, the capitalists, the billionaires, the bourgeoisie, are deadlocked. The middle class, the petty bourgeois, are now behind the proletariat. Now is the time to mount an insurrection. The women are leading the revolution. They alone are capable of organizing the insurrection. Trump is planning a return to power. The country is counting on you. There is no time to waste. Strike now. Let the slogans be:

Scientific Socialism!

Victory or Death!

Fight Like A Girl!

Dictatorship Of the Proletariat!

Anarchy: A Real Possibility

Jul 9, 2021

The current crisis in capitalism, which has been intensified by the Corona Virus, has led to widespread unemployment, homelessness, hunger, drug abuse and gun violence, due to a sense of desperation and despair. The press reports that over the July 4 long weekend alone, 233 people were shot dead. These are politely referred to as "mass casualty events". On average, there are 54 people who are shot and killed in America *each day!* The experts expect a "dramatic increase in gun violence" over the summer months.

In addition, the restrictions on travel and gatherings, which have been used so effectively against the virus, are being eased. Under certain conditions, face masks are no longer required. Public gatherings are once again taking place. Bars and restaurants are reopening. The airlines are once again doing a booming business, or at least this holiday weekend.

Yet the virus has mutated, to a new, more "hypertransmissable" strain, (the adjective is not mine), referred to as the "Delta" variant. This has given rise to a "ten percent" increase in the daily infection rate, so that the country is seeing the highest daily rate of infections since April. If this trend continues, then we can anticipate that the virus will return, with a vengeance.

It is clear that the government leaders in Washington, our democratically elected officials, are not losing any sleep over such little details. They are preoccupied with the "Big Lie", as well as the "January 6 Insurrection". The two are related, two sides of the same coin. The Big Lie is a none too subtle reference to the belief, among millions of Americans, that Trump won the presidential election, so that Biden is an imposter president.

The demonstration in the capital of Washington, on January 6, in which protesters occupied the government building of the Congress, is being referred to as an "Insurrection". Those protesters are being referred to as anarchists, which they are not. They are devoted followers of Trump, convinced that he is the true president, and want him placed back in the White House.

This stands in stark contrast to anarchists, who want no government.

The bourgeois politicians have their priorities well established. The death of so many Americans, due to the Corona Virus, now well over 600,000 and rising, as well as the shooting deaths of thousands more, do not concern them. Their only concern is that of maintaining the power of the capitalists, the billionaires, the bourgeoisie.

Their fears are well grounded. It is entirely possible that Trump did indeed win the last presidential election, if only because of an archaic system, in the form of the Electoral College. As we have gone into this in another article, there is no need to repeat it. Suffice it to say that it is not the citizens who elect the president, but the members of the Electoral College. Falsifying those election results is simplicity itself.

The manner in which elections are falsified was documented, quite clearly, by the former personal lawyer for Trump, Rudy Giuliani. It was a valuable public service, and revealed one of the methods of rule, of the capitalists. As a "reward" for this public service, he is now no longer allowed to practice law in the state of New York.

As for those who took part in the largely peaceful protests of January 6, in Washington, hundreds have been arrested and charged with very serious crimes.

The capitalists, the bourgeoisie, consider Trump and his followers to be a threat to their authority, as indeed they are. They are concerned with maintaining their rule, rather than the death and destruction caused by the Virus and gun violence.

As was documented in a previous article, the collapse of a rather large apartment building in Florida is cause for great concern, as it draws attention to the fact that the infrastructure of the country is in desperate need of repair. Without those repairs, we can expect the collapse of more buildings, as well as bridges and tunnels. Our roads and highways are also in desperate need of repair. At the same time, the sewage, electric and telecommunication systems are also on the verge of collapse. But as was pointed out previously, according to an article in Business Insider, the capitalists are afraid that such repairs would strengthen the working class, and "enable workers to demand higher wages and force the wealthy to pay a fairer share of taxes". Those repairs are not about to take place. The capitalists are prepared to allow the country to sink to the level of underdeveloped countries, of the so called "third world", rather than pay more taxes.

The capitalists are about to find out that there are limits, to that which working people are about to tolerate. Those limits are rapidly being approached.

The latest episode in the "gong show", the "soap opera", which is currently referred to as America, is the release from prison of a man who was a convicted sex offender. He was released on a technicality, and not because he was innocent. Yet he is also a "celebrity", a well known comedian, and of course quite wealthy. For that reason, he was able to hire expensive lawyers, and they were able to secure his release, upon appeal.

No doubt, this has added to the bitterness and frustration of countless American women, especially those who claim that this same "skinner" (as that is the popular name of sex offenders) has also raped them. In fact, possibly fifty women have come forward with this accusation, and very likely there are a great many others. Many women, who have been raped, dare not come forward, if only due to the social stigma involved with being raped. Sad but true.

As well, at the end of this month, the moratorium on housing evictions will be ended. At that time, possibly seven million Americans will face eviction, and will be forced to join the ranks of the homeless.

So many desperate people, with no place to turn. All government agencies serve the same class, the capitalists, the bourgeois. The only people who care about working people, are other working people. For that reason, anarchy is a distinct possibility.

A similar situation took place in 1917 Russia, immediately after the February revolution, in which the Czar was overthrown. The capitalists, the bourgeoisie, were then able to seize power.

Yet the common people, by whom we mean the workers and peasants, had formed Soviets, or in English, Councils, and had considerable power. There were Soviets of Workers, Peasants and Soldiers. The problem was that they were voluntarily surrendering their power to the capitalists. This too, gave rise to the threat of anarchy.

Of course, Lenin was appalled by this, properly so. It made the necessity for revolution ever more urgent. For that reason, among others, the Central Committee of the Communist Party decided to mount an Insurrection, in the interests of seizing political power, so as to establish the Dictatorship Of the Proletariat.

In fact, that Insurrection happened on November 7, new style calendar, or October 25, old style calendar. For that reason it is called the "October Revolution", and it brought the common people, the workers and poor peasants, to power.

By contrast, there is currently no Marxist political party in America, which is to say no Communist Party, one which calls for the Dictatorship Of the Proletariat. Yet that is a rather minor detail which can be easily remedied, now that we are blessed with the Internet. We also have no shortage of middle class intellectuals, those who are familiar with the revolutionary theories of Marx and Lenin. More accurately, former members of the middle class. The virus has served to accelerate the course of world history, so that countless members of the middle class have been ruined, forced into the ranks of the working class. Welcome, my brothers and sisters, my comrades! As you are aware of those revolutionary theories, and you have impressive computer skills, you can quickly form a proper Communist Party, Dictatorship Of the Proletariat.

Then, it is a rather simple matter of organizing an Insurrection, as happened on November 7, 1917, in Russia. Bear in mind that the events of January 6, 2021, in Washington, has exposed the weakness of the capitalists. The capital is practically unguarded!

Now, here in America, "Autonomous Zones" are being established. These are the American equivalent of Soviets, or Councils. People have learned to not stake out geographical areas, as that results in the assault of government forces, in overwhelming numbers. This happened in Seattle. Instead, such "Zones" are being established, as parts of cities or whole towns, and should be encouraged. The members of those Zones should learn to use firearms, at least twenty twos. Both male and female. Such rifles are quite inexpensive, and the ammunition is far less expensive than that of high powered rifles. The impact on the shoulder is also quite manageable.

American women have proven themselves to be excellent organizers, as was proven by the Womens' March on Washington. Ladies, you have done it before, you can do it again. Only this time, no half measures. Go for broke. Seize political power. January 6 was not an "Insurrection", as the capitalists claim. Let them know precisely the meaning of the word Insurrection!

We do not need anarchy. We need socialism, in the form of the Dictatorship Of the Proletariat. Now is the time for Insurrection.

Ladies: Socialism or Anarchy-Your Choice!

Jul 28, 2021

The current crisis in capitalism is continuing to intensify. The Covid 19 virus, which was thought to be under control, has apparently managed to mutate to a more deadly strain, referred to as the Delta variation. In a very short time, it has spread across the country and the infection rates are sky rocketing. In addition, gun violence, referred to as "mass casualty events", in which more than one person is killed or wounded, are now almost routine. It is just a matter of time before the system breaks down completely. At some point, both the medical and the law enforcement agencies will collapse. At that time, the country will be facing anarchy. No law. Survival of the fittest. Gangs of people with guns will be roaming at will, raping and looting as they please.

As for those who think that I am overstating the situation, feel free to face the fact that such events have happened before. At the time of the collapse of a civilization, a period of anarchy always takes place. The American civilization is close to collapse.

The one and only alternative is socialism, by which I mean scientific socialism, as all forms of utopian socialism simply do not work. Of course I am referring to the Dictatorship Of the Proletariat, a fundamental tenet of Marxism. It is also the worst night mare of all dedicated capitalists. With good reason, I might add.

In opposition to those forces of reaction, that of the capitalists, we have the progressive forces, which have given rise to the movement of the "Autonomous Zones". The experience of the Seattle Autonomous Zone, which was crushed with considerable brutality, has taught people that such Zones can never be completely autonomous. The capitalists see these Zones as a dual power, as indeed they are, a threat to the rule of capital, that of the bourgeoisie. For that reason, they are determined to crush all such Zones. The working people have responded by establishing Zones, areas of influence within cities and towns, while not kidding themselves that such Zones are autonomous. At least, under capitalism, they can never be autonomous.

Now these Zones have to be united, organized into a vast network, a country wide network of working people. Within each Zone, the members have to be trained in the use of various weapons, including clubs, shields, helmets, paint balls, tasers, slings and firearms. Marxist literature must be made available, especially that of State and Revolution, by Lenin. That is the work which is most relevant. Another American revolution is fast approaching, and working people had best be prepared.

Recent experience has revealed that the only people who are capable of organizing, at least on a nation wide scale, are the American women. Within the space of a few weeks, from the time Trump was elected to the presidency, to the time he was sworn into office, the women organized a nation wide protest. It was possibly the largest, most successful protest movement in the country. Now is the time to build upon that success, to carry the revolution through to its logical conclusion, that of scientific socialism.

The events of January 6 of this year, in the capitol of the nation, referred to as the "one six insurrection", have revealed that the headquarters of the capitalists, the vipers nest of American imperialism, is no where near as well guarded as we would expect. It is clear that a well organized insurrection could succeed in overthrowing the government, possibly with very little blood shed.

At that point, after the insurrection, many people taking part in the revolution will no doubt insist on taking over the existing state apparatus, and setting themselves up as the new rulers. That is the reason State and Revolution is so important, as it stresses the importance of *smashing* the existing state machine and replacing it with a new, proletarian state apparatus, in order to crush the "desperate and determined" resistance of the capitalists, the bourgeoisie, as they make every effort to restore their "paradise lost". This new state apparatus is referred to as the *Dictatorship Of the Proletariat!*

As for those who scoff at the idea of studying that most essential work of Lenin, bear in mind the advice of Engels, who stated that "*without a revolutionary theory, there can be no revolutionary movement*"*!* Further bear in mind that the working class is not class conscious, not aware of itself as a class, with its own class interests, and that this consciousness has to be brought to the working class, from an outside source. That outside source is bourgeois intellectuals. The fact that working class people are rising up, demanding change, does not imply class consciousness. It merely represents "consciousness in an *embryonic form*", as Lenin explained quite clearly in his work, What Is To Be Done? That is another Marxist work that deserves careful study.

With that in mind, I can also suggest that all working people join the two mainstream political parties, Democrat and Republican, as card carrying members. It is such members who determine the candidates for all political offices, and in fact they set policy. No doubt the capitalists will see this as a threat to their base of power, and change their method of rule. In this manner, the working people will learn, from their own experience, that the Marxists are right. The capitalists are in charge, they rule, and fully intend to continue to rule. A revolution is required to dislodge them.

The fact is that people need leaders, and the only proper working class leaders are the true Marxists, those who call for the Dictatorship Of the Proletariat. Lenin refers to this as the "touchstone" of a Marxist. For that reason, it is essential to create an American Communist Party, Dictatorship Of the Proletariat, ACP, DOP. Of course, it has to be exclusive, limited to the true Marxists.

In conclusion, may I suggest that the American ladies have their work cut out for them. They have got to learn the ways of the warrior, and that includes the use of firearms. They also have to organize a nation wide network of working people, bringing together the various Zones. All members must be trained in the use of weapons. Preparations must be made for an insurrection, in which the proletariat seizes political power.

As well, all members should be encouraged to read the most essential works of Marx and Lenin. Young and old should also be encouraged to join the two parties, to take part in "changing the system from within". (As if that is about to happen!) Then there is the not so little matter of forming an American Communist Party, Dictatorship Of the Proletariat.

Without doubt, that is a tall order. Yet it is necessary to prepare for the Dictatorship Of the Proletariat. If properly prepared, the revolution, and especially the insurrection, can be quick and painless, almost bloodless. The alternative is anarchy.

Capitalist Opposition to Infrastructure Repair

Jul 1, 2021

Recently in Florida, a twelve story apartment building collapsed, killing a great many people. The press is covering this story very closely, properly so. They are also reporting that this collapse raises a great many questions concerning the integrity of other buildings, as well as the infrastructure of the whole country. In this they are correct, so perhaps it is best to explain these terms.

The building in question was over forty years old and constructed with concrete, which was reinforced with steel bar. That steel bar is referred to as rebar, which is short for reinforced bar. This rebar gives the concrete more strength. The press also reports that the concrete on the building was "spalling", or cracking, and that this cracking is an indication that the steel rebar is rusting.

Of course the collapse of this building raises the question of the safety of other buildings, especially those which are greater than forty years old. It also raises the question of the safety of the infrastructure of the whole country. The press was also quick to point this out, without explaining the meaning of the term infrastructure.

Perhaps someone should explain to the journalists, that not everyone who watches the news is a cross between a Philadelphia lawyer and a mechanical engineer. With that in mind, we will mention that, according to the internet, the infrastructure is a reference to "the basic physical and organizational structures and facilities, such as bridges, roads, power supplies and tunnels, needed for the operation of a society." They go on to mention that this includes the water and sewage network. Now we know.

This is certainly a legitimate concern, as many of those structures were built a great many years ago. It stands to reason that without proper routine maintenance, it is just a matter of time before they fall apart. Yet maintenance costs money, and the capitalists have been cutting back on such expenses for many years. It follows that a great many more buildings are about to collapse, and not just apartment complexes.

It only makes sense to repair the infrastructure of the country, before it falls apart, in the interest of keeping the country running smoothly, as well as for the sake of safety. This would also help to put countless people to work, performing vital repairs, and in the process, being paid for this, quite handsomely. This would help to stimulate the economy, and in fact, Senator Bernie Sanders has recently proposed a six trillion dollar stimulus package, for those repairs. Yet the capitalists are opposed to this.

Recently, in one of the most respected publications of the capitalists (respected by the capitalists), they revealed their thought processes, to put it politely. To put it more accurately, they revealed their absolute stupidity and total disregard for human life. As they phrased it:

"Crises have a tendency to kill old orthodoxies and usher in new ones. The horrors of the Great Depression galvanized governments to start fighting recessions, instead of waiting for the market to work itself out . . . *It is better to overdue it on stimulus than to under do it,* economists concluded, *next time we'll prime the economy with the mother of all pumps". (*italics by the capitalists)

The article went on to sing the praises of perhaps the finest of the bourgeois economists, John Maynard Keynes. He was active in the early twentieth century. Yet even though he was admired by the capitalists, at no time did they ever take his advice.

At the end of the First World War, it was Keynes who advised the Allies to cancel all debts. They did not. Instead, at the Treaty of Versailles, the Allies imposed staggering war reparations on Germany. As Keynes put it, this was sure to lead to "serious economic and political repercussions on Europe and the world". He was so right.

Now to return to the same article:

"That's exactly what happened when the greatest crisis of the century (the twenty first century) came crashing down. Congress approved trillions of dollars in Covid relief . . . It was the kind of government activism that would have stunned even John Maynard Keynes . . . A little over a year into the crisis, the preliminary results of those actions are in, and they're phenomenal. The US economy is on track this year to grow at its fastest pace since 1984 . . . they could put millions of Americans to work . . . It's Keynes on steroids"

So far so good. They finally took the advice of their own bourgeois expert, an economist, and were amazed by the results. But now comes the kicker:

"But . . . A growing chorus of voices . . . fear that government spending . . . *would enable the workers to demand higher wages and force the wealthy to pay a fairer share of taxes*". (my italics)

There we have it. The capitalists are afraid that if they invest too much money in infrastructure maintenance and repairs, then the standard of living of the working class will rise, the working class will become ever stronger, they will force the capitalists to increase the wages, and even force the capitalists to "pay a fairer share of taxes". Better to allow the infrastructure of the country to fall apart, rather than pay the workers higher wages and pay higher taxes!

Without doubt, the capitalists, and especially the bourgeois economists, are supremely well aware of the theories of Marx. They even admit, in private, that Marx was correct. That in no way changes the fact that they are going to do everything in their power to further enrich themselves, at the expense of the working class, of course. If that means running the country into the ground, so be it.

They are very likely aware that it was Marx who stated that "reforms are a byproduct of revolutionary motion". He went on to say that those reforms "strengthen and further the revolutionary motion". As the repairs of the infrastructure of the country amounts to a reform, the capitalists are opposed to this. They are aware that it would strengthen and further the revolutionary motion.

They see such repairs as a threat to their way of life. It could result in an increase of wages for the working class, as well as an increase in taxes for the capitalists. As far as the capitalists are concerned, it is better to allow the country to fall apart, starting with the infrastructure.

We live under monopoly capitalism, which is imperialism. As Lenin pointed out, imperialism is completely reactionary. This is just one more example of such reaction.

National Liberation and Collapse of the American Empire

Jun 7, 2021

The revolutionary motion in America continues to intensify. The journalists are reporting that since the beginning of the year, there have been over two hundred fifty mass shootings in the country. There were ten mass shootings last weekend alone. As well, a federal court has just struck down a California law, banning assault rifles. The sense of desperation within the country is being transformed, into a sense of despair. Even the most distinguished politicians are expressing the fear that their democracy is about to collapse.

Indeed, their democracy is about to collapse, the democracy of the capitalists, the bourgeois. It is bourgeois democracy, a democracy of the capitalists, by the capitalists, for the capitalists. It is about to be replaced by a new democracy, a proletarian democracy, a democracy of the proletariat, by the proletariat, for the proletariat. For the capitalists, the billionaires, the bourgeoisie, it will be a dictatorship. A Dictatorship Of the Proletariat.

It is up to conscious people, those who are aware of the revolutionary theories of Marx and Lenin, to make working people, the proletariat, aware of themselves as a class, with interests which are diametrically opposed to the interests of the capitalists, the bourgeoisie. The working class is destined to overthrow the capitalists and establish scientific socialism, in the form of the Dictatorship Of the Proletariat. As yet, they are just not aware of this.

The country can best be thought of as a "powder key", in that any spark can cause an explosion. That is bound to give rise to a spontaneous uprising. What we need is a conscious uprising.

With that in mind, it is best to mention that, for perhaps the first time in history, the revolutionary movement for national liberation may coincide with the revolutionary movement for scientific socialism. The two together may well bring down a modern empire, the American empire, and at the same time, establish a number of independent socialist republics.

The combination of the Second Great Depression and the Corona Virus has served to accelerate the course of world history. It has given rise to crises, such as have not been seen since the nineteen thirties. In America, the number of unemployed is at a level not seen since the Great Depression. Countless people are homeless, sleeping on the streets and under bridges. The "more fortunate" are able to live in vehicles. Millions of others are waiting for the temporary ban on evictions to expire, after which they too, will be evicted. The extra burden of bankruptcy will then be added to their miserable lives.

Yet the American working class, the proletariat, is exceptionally revolutionary, even though they are not aware of this. They have been well educated in the class struggle. Starting in the sixties of the last century, various movements grew and developed. The strongest was the Viet Nam Anti War movement, which reached a peak in 1969. A march on Washington was organized, and on November 15 of that year, the press estimated that half a million protesters marched on the capital. Within the city, all of the bureaucrats and politicians were convinced that the only thing that stopped the protesters from "taking over", was the fact that they had no leaders. In this, they were correct.

In 1970, every university in the country went on strike. Then the revolutionary motion died down, and of course reaction set in, as it always does. There followed many years in which the working class was in "orderly retreat", as it were. Many years later, the revolutionary motion picked up, in the form of the Occupy

Movement. A whole new generation of Americans learned first hand, that the capitalists are in charge, and fully intend to remain in charge. At that time, among the protesters, there was a vague sense of the existence of classes, in that they referred to the "one percent", as opposed to themselves, the "ninety nine percent". No signs or banners contained any class content. There was no reference to the bourgeoisie, or the proletariat. But then the protesters were not aware of those classes.

Just as the Anti War movement was crushed, so too the Occupy Movement was crushed. The police responded with clubs, shields, tear gas, pepper spray and water cannons. The tents of the peaceful protesters were torn down, and countless people were thrown in jail. A new generation learned that their democratically elected leaders were well aware of the "inequalities" within the system. The efforts of the protesters to explain to the politicians, that the system was not working properly, fell on deaf ears. They learned that the system was working precisely the way it was supposed to work. The system, that of the dictatorship of the bourgeoisie, protects the bourgeoisie.

The protesters who were young, received a rude awakening. The older protesters, and there were a considerable number of them, were not surprised. All emerged from the struggle as veterans. The only difference was that the young ones became tempered.

Many of those same veterans are now taking part in the Autonomous Zone movement. They are aware that to occupy part of a city merely results in an attack, by an overpowering force. So now the Zones are being set up, but not in the geographical sense. Yet progress has been made, in that the protesters are no longer making any reference to the "one percent", as opposed to the "ninety nine percent". The working class is moving closer to class consciousness.

The working class, the proletariat, can only go so far. They are not aware that they are destined to overthrow the capitalists, the bourgeoisie, and to crush them under the Dictatorship Of the Proletariat. It is up to class conscious intellectuals to make the proletariat aware of this.

The working class should also be made aware of the fact that the capitalists have set up a state apparatus, or a government, to which it is generally referred, for the purpose of crushing the working class, the proletariat. Elections are a mere formality, in which the working class gets to choose the particular members of the bourgeois, to go to the various capitols and misrepresent the working class.

As most intellectuals are middle class, it is their duty to explain this to the working class, the proletariat. Bear in mind that both Marx and Lenin were middle class intellectuals. Now, as a result of the twin crises in capitalism, the middle class, the petty bourgeois, is being ruined. Countless members of the middle class, including intellectuals, are being forced into the ranks of the proletariat, and they bring with them the awareness of the revolutionary theories of Marx and Lenin.

The American working class is now instinctively gravitating towards socialism, while at the same time gravitating towards national liberation. Truly remarkable. Several republics have already taken shape, and no doubt, others will follow, and very soon. Then at the time of the insurrection, the American government will be overthrown, the American empire will collapse, and a number of independent socialist republics will come into existence.

In 1917 Russia, the Socialist Soviet Russian Republic was first formed, and only several years later, did other socialist republics come together to form the Soviet Union.

The burden on the people who are organizing the insurrection, just became greater. They not only have to plan a nation wide insurrection, but also plan to establish a number of socialist republics, immediately after the successful insurrection. Further, it is quite likely that the revolution will cross borders, into Canada and possibly Mexico.

Lest people scoff, bear in mind that New England has recently broken in two. The southern three states of Massachusetts, Connecticut and Rhode Island, have joined with the states of New York, New Jersey, Pennsylvania and Delaware. The northern three states, that of Maine, Vermont and New Hampshire, could very well join with the Canadian Maritime Provinces, that of New Brunswick, Nova Scotia and Prince Edward Island. They have a great deal in common. Further, Alaska could separate and join with the Canadian Yukon, for example. These are merely a couple of examples, and no doubt, the people who live in those areas, as well as a great many others, will decide their own future.

Never before has a revolution on this scale taken shape. Yet never before has a working class, the proletariat, been so schooled in the class struggle. So many of them are now seasoned veterans, ready to take up arms against their class enemies, the capitalists, the billionaires, the bourgeoisie. The only thing lacking now is the leaders.

With that in mind, my message, to so many former members of the middle class, is that I suggest you cast aside your illusions. Your previous life style is gone, never to return. Your years of faithful service, to the bourgeoisie, count for nothing. Expect no reward. Do not look back. Forward!

Focus now on building a new society, a proletarian society. Your knowledge and skills are needed. Take part in the creation of a proper Communist Party, Dictatorship Of the Proletariat.

Bring to the working class the consciousness they so desperately need. Take a leading role in the revolution. After the revolution, after the capitalists are crushed under the Dictatorship Of the Proletariat, professional people will be in demand. They will be paid most handsomely. Do not get mad. Get even!

We will know that our message is getting through when the banners and posters read:

Scientific Socialism!

Dictatorship Of the Proletariat!

Workers of the World, Unite!

Support Bernie Sanders!

Jul 14, 2021

There is only one Senator who is calling for a massive improvement to the infrastructure of the country, and that is the Independent Senator from the state of Vermont, the self described Independent Socialist, Bernie Sanders. He is now Chairman of the powerful Senate Budget Committee, and is not satisfied with the *3.5 trillion dollar* infrastructure package in domestic investments. Sanders is arguing that *6 trillion dollars* is required!

It is clear that Senator Sanders is a devoted follower of John Maynard Keynes, one of the most highly respected bourgeois economists of the twentieth century. As the current bourgeois economists phrase it, "the main plank of Keynes's theory, which has come to bear his name, is the assertion that aggregate demand -measured as the sum of spending by households, businesses and the government- is the most important driving force of an economy".

To think that the bourgeois economist who came up with that "plank", is considered to be one of the best and brightest! What else could "demand" be, but the "spending of households, businesses and government"? And how could that not be the "most important driving force of the economy"? Yet Keynes is considered to be a genius for pointing this out!

Perhaps it would be best to allow Sanders to explain this in his own words, as he expressed himself after meeting with President Biden. "He knows and I know that we're seeing an economy where the very, very rich are getting richer, while working families are struggling . . . My job is to do everything I can to see that the Senate comes forward with the strongest possible legislation to protect the needs of the working families of this country . . .

We want to see a reconciliation bill which shows the working families of this country that the government can and must work for them. What we are trying to do is transformative. The legislation that the president and I are supporting will go further to improve the lives of working people than any legislation since the 1930's . . . Does anyone deny that our child care system, for example, is a disaster? Does anyone deny that pre K, similarly, is totally inadequate? Does anyone deny that there's something absurd that our young people can't afford to go to college, or are leaving school deeply in debt? Does anyone deny that our infrastructure is collapsing?"

Well spoken, Bernie Sanders! No one can deny that!

It is clear that Sanders is one of the finest "Independent Socialists", technically referred to as a utopian socialist. He has stated the problem clearly, while carefully avoiding any reference to classes. The "very, very rich" is a reference to the billionaires, the bourgeoisie, and he is correct that they are "getting richer". The "working families" is a reference to the working class, the proletariat, and it is true that the working class is "struggling". Or at best, many of the working people are struggling, while so many others are unemployed, homeless, hungry and desperate. In fact, these people are not so much struggling, as being degraded.

As a result of the revolutionary motion that is sweeping the country, Senator Sanders has been placed in charge of the powerful Senate Budget Committee. As such, he is correct when he states that it is his duty to "protect the needs of the working families of this country". For that reason, he is proposing a massive "reconciliation bill", with the idea of providing proper education, from pre kindergarten through college, along with a major overhaul of the infrastructure, among other things. What is more, he thinks that President Biden supports him on this. Now where would he get an idea like that? Probably from President Biden, as a means of stalling Sanders!

The fact of the matter is that many of the finest intellectuals among the capitalists, especially the economists, are well aware of the revolutionary theories of Marx and Lenin. What is more, they are also well aware that those theories are correct. All the more reason to do everything in their power to divert the revolutionary motion!

Those same bourgeois economists are well aware that, as Marx stated, "reforms serve to strengthen and further the revolutionary motion". For that reason, they are opposed to reforms. They tried to block the recent "economic stimulation package", in which almost all Americans received a "stimie check", and it worked wonders for the economy. It also served to "strengthen and further the revolutionary motion", as the bourgeois economists are well aware. They are afraid that the proposed "reconciliation bill" will do even more damage, to the extent of workers demanding higher wages, as well as forcing the billionaires, the bourgeoisie, to pay a higher rate of taxes. God forbid!

Yet the fact remains that the "stimie checks" have served to strengthen the working class revolutionary motion, and it is time to build upon that. The best way to do that is by having all "Leftist" people come together in support of Senator Sanders. It matters not if they consider themselves to be Independent Socialists, Democratic Socialists, Social Democrats, Communists or just plain socialists. For that matter, they can be anarchists or people who are determined to see some change for the better. We can all agree to support Sanders, in his quest to force through the "reconciliation bill".

Perhaps the best way to do this is to join the two mainstream political parties, both Democrat and Republican, as card carrying members. As such members decide the candidates for all political offices, they have great power. They can force elected officials to vote in favour of Sanders and his reconciliation bill, because if they do not, they will not be allowed to run for reelection. Faced with the prospect of career suicide, watch how fast they become sweetly reasonable!

At the same time, the true Communists, those who call for the Dictatorship Of the Proletariat, can use that platform to make clear that the problem is one of capitalism, that the capitalists, the bourgeoisie, must be overthrown and crushed under the Dictatorship Of the Bourgeoisie. In this way, we can distinguish ourselves from the social chauvinists and the utopian socialists. Bear in mind that our goal is to raise the level of awareness of the working class. The one and only way to overthrow the capitalists is by abolishing the existing state apparatus. As well, we can possibly persuade the utopian socialists of the correctness of our policies, while making clear our differences with the social chauvinists.

We are suggesting this as a course of action, in conjunction with the creation of a Communist Party, Dictatorship Of the Proletariat. As well, the members of the various Zones, which have sprung up across the country, should prepare for the insurrection. That includes learning the proper use of firearms, especially twenty twos, as they are the least expensive. As well, both men and women should learn to use night sticks, pepper spray, paint balls and slings, complete with marbles. Become comfortable with the wearing of helmets and bullet proof vests. Each Zone should be provided with several pipe wrenches, and all should be taught to use them. Opening up a fire hydrant is simplicity itself. If enough hydrants are opened, the water pressure drops to zero, and the use of water cannons is neutralized, as the water trucks get their water from fire hydrants.

As the American women are currently leading the revolutionary motion, this falls mainly upon their shoulders. The women have proven themselves to be excellent organizers, and those are precisely the skills we need now. It was Lenin who consistently stressed the importance of the "key link". The key link now is organization, in preparation for the Dictatorship Of the Proletariat. Ladies, we have complete confidence in you.

Tasks of the Proletariat and of the Intellectuals

Jun 10, 2021

The combination of the Corona Virus pandemic and of the Second Great Depression has caused a crisis in capitalism, such as has not been seen since the First Great Depression, of the nineteen thirties. Under such extreme pressure, caused by unemployment, homelessness, hunger and desperation, a great many people are "cracking" under the strain, resorting to acts of senseless violence. The sense of desperation that has recently gripped the nation is being transformed, into a sense of despair. So many people are prepared to "throw in the towel"! Now the attitude is one of "what is the use?"

Yet it is characteristic that, under extreme pressure, some people are broken, while others rise to the occasion. It may bring out the best in some people. Now we are in a time of revolutionary motion, in that countless members of the working class, those whom were formerly apathetic, are now politically active. These are the advanced workers, the more enlightened members of the working class, the proletariat. It is important to bear in mind that the proletariat is no different from any other group of people, in that they listen to their own, the people they respect. The less advanced, broad mass of workers listen closely to the more advanced.

The American proletariat has now gone about as far as it can, on its own. Different groups are demanding different reforms. Black Lives Matter is demanding an end to violent police repression. Me Too is demanding an end to sexual assaults. The Autonomous Zone movement is demanding various reform. Across the country, people are calling for different reforms. Now it is up to socialist intellectuals to do their part.

It is the intellectuals who are aware of the revolutionary theories of Marx and Lenin. The proletariat are not aware of those theories. It is up to these intellectuals, to bring to the working class the awareness of those revolutionary theories. At the same time, the workers must be respected. The vast majority of them are honest, hard working, law abiding citizens. They have been bombarded with bourgeois propaganda all their lives. It is only natural that they should believe that which they have been told. The workers have to learn, from their own experience, that the capitalists are a pack of liars.

To counteract the capitalist propaganda, may I suggest that we take the capitalists at their word. The capitalists say that if we do not like the way things are, then we should "change the system from within". Excellent idea.

With that in mind, may I suggest that all Independent Socialists, Social Democrats, Democratic Socialists or just plain Socialists, get together and join the two mainstream political parties, both Democrat and Republican, as card carrying members. Now is not the time to be shy. I can further suggest that you encourage all of your relatives and friends to also join the two parties. No doubt all of you are aware of the revolutionary theories of Marx and Lenin. You may or may not agree with them. Either way, is perfectly acceptable. We do not have to be in complete agreement, in order to work together. Equally without doubt, all American Socialists are well aware that the Constitution guarantees the right to "life, liberty and the pursuit of happiness". Go for it!

As card carrying members of the two parties, Democrat and Republican, you can suggest a new political platform. Certain fundamental human rights should be guaranteed, such as medical, education, freedom from hunger, adequate housing and the right to live a life of dignity. With that in mind, may I suggest:

1. Free medical for all, including emergency services, hospitalizations, home care and medications

2. Free education for all, no tuition, cancel all student loans

3. Free and nutritions food for all

4. Free housing for all, the abandoned buildings to be converted into housing

5. Cancellation of the national debt

6. Pensions for seniors to be tax free

7. Graduated income tax, with the rich paying their fair share

8. Military training for all able bodied people, both male and female, over the age of 16

9. People with such training to take over the role of the police and National Guard, on a part time basis, with the days worked to be paid for, by the employer

10. All elected officials to be subject to recall at any time, and paid the wages of workers

11. All banks in the country to be amalgamated, and put under workers control

12. All prisons to be shut down, the inmates to be put to work

No doubt many Socialist may think that this platform does not have a “hope in hell” of being carried out. To such skeptics, I can only respond that you are so right! The idea is to raise the level of awareness of the working class, the vast majority of whom have been misled by the capitalists. There is no way that the party bosses, of either party, are going to allow countless working people to join their party, and "take over". Instead, they will attempt to change their method of rule. In the process, they will expose themselves to the working people, the proletariat, as the liars and swindlers, that they are.

The true Marxists, Communists, those who call for the Dictatorship Of the Proletariat -as that is the touchstone of a true Communist- must work with the utopian socialists, as we have no quarrel with them, while making clear that we are convinced that the capitalists, the billionaires, the bourgeoisie, must be overthrown and crushed, under the Dictatorship Of the Proletariat.

At the same time, we must also make it clear that we have a real problem with those who claim to be Marxists, but deny the necessity for the Dictatorship Of the Proletariat. We want nothing to do with such social chauvinists. Yet we cannot avoid marches and demonstrations, just because the social chauvinists are there. We can distinguish ourselves by proudly bearing signs and banners which call for the Dictatorship Of the Proletariat.

Of course the capitalists will make every effort to block any worker, or socialist, from running for any political office. Yet it is reasonable to assume that some people will manage to run for office, as a Democrat, Republican or even as a Socialist. The important thing is not that they should win, but that the message should be made clear.

We should encourage working people to choose candidates for any and all political office, preferably one of their own. Then again, if they insist that a Communist should run for office, so be it. At the time of the revolution, such people, placed in Washington, may prove to be quite useful.

Then again, should the workers choose candidates who are utopian socialists, that too is fine. In the process of going to Washington, and trying to change things, they and their constituency will learn that the capitalists are in charge, and fully intend to remain in charge.

The main thing to bear in mind, is that the goal is to raise the level of awareness of the working class, the proletariat. It is not a numbers game. If we succeed in sending a few people to Washington, fine. If not, that is also fine. The important thing is that our policy is correct. Merely making the working class aware of our socialist program, is a step in the right direction. No doubt the capitalists will make it most emphatically clear, to the working people, that there is no chance that they are going to get free medical, education or housing! There is still less chance of the capitalists paying their fair share of taxes!

This will help to drive the point home, to the working class, that we are right. From their own experience, they will come to realize that the capitalists, the billionaires, the bourgeoisie, are completely reactionary. Truly, they must be overthrown and crushed, under the Dictatorship Of the Proletariat.

www.ingramcontent.com/pod-product-compliance
Lightning Source LLC
Chambersburg PA
CBHW060255030426
42335CB00014B/1712

* 9 7 8 1 9 5 2 3 0 2 7 4 9 *